Focus on the SEASONS

Focus on FALL

By Rosie Seaman

Fearon Teacher Aids
Simon & Schuster Supplementary Education Group

ABOUT THE AUTHOR

Rosie Seaman is an educator, author, and television producer. She has written several books for children and her work has been highlighted in a number of national magazines. As director of children's programming for WKRG-TV in Mobile, Alabama, Ms. Seaman has developed a variety of educational programs for young children.

Ms. Seaman received her certification in the Montessori method of preschool education and bases her work on the Montessori philosophy that young children learn best through techniques that encourage manipulation, experimentation, and discovery of the world around them.

Editorial Director: Virginia L. Murphy

Editors: Marilyn Trow and Sue Mogard

Copyeditor: Lisa Schwimmer

Design: Terry McGrath

Production: Rebecca Speakes

Cover Design: Lucyna Green

Cover and Inside Illustration: Marilynn Barr

ISBN 0-86653-973-5

Contents

A Note from the Author

The *Focus on the Seasons* series teaches basic skills, concepts, and subject matter to young children through active participation and discovery. Arranged in four seasonal books, the activities offer young learners the opportunity to express themselves freely throughout the school year as they contribute to their school environment.

Focus on Fall helps children discover some of the seasonal changes of this exciting season. Children learn more about themselves and the world around them, discover new friends, explore fall through their senses as well as through art, and celebrate Halloween and Thanksgiving.

Invite the children to help set up an area in the classroom for sharing completed projects about fall. For example, a specific wall space and table may be used to display the children's creations. Displaying children's work is important to reinforce visually the skills and concepts they learn each day.

Use this book as a way of opening many other exciting avenues for exploring fall with the children. The results will be an accumulation of endless treasures that will always be of great value to both you and your young students. Have fun together!

Rosie Seaman

Introduction

The *Focus on the Seasons* series encourages you, the teacher, to be actively involved with the children and their learning. Each seasonal book provides children with an opportunity to learn about the seasons, as well as one another, through hands-on experiences with a variety of materials.

The format of each book offers easy reference to activities that explore commonly used early-childhood units, as well as suggesting a hands-on approach for implementing the activities into existing programs. Each book presents simple directions and bold illustrations and includes a bibliography of quality children's books to enhance the seasonal themes.

The activities begin with a list of materials to gather and offer suggested discussion questions. Each activity provides a step-by-step process for involving the children and suggests other alternatives when appropriate.

A SUGGESTED APPROACH

Prior to each activity:

➤ invite the children into the activity with the discussion questions, expanding the ideas presented in the questions as the children show interest.

➤ display the suggested materials on a low table in a work area that encourages the children to work independently.

During each activity:

➤ encourage the children to express their unique ideas through the materials.

➤ become involved with the children through conversations or mutual participation in the projects.

Following each activity:

➤ place the materials in a learning center in the classroom for the children to explore during independent time.

➤ display the children's completed creations in the classroom for you and the children to enjoy.

OBSERVING THE CHANGES OF FALL

FALL is a season filled with many changes. Through hands-on activities, the children will explore seasonal changes of trees, discover fruits and vegetables that are harvested in the fall, and learn about fall flowers and insects.

Leaf Rubbings

MATERIALS

➤ fallen leaves (oak, maple, chestnut, and so on)

➤ white drawing paper

➤ paperless crayons

SHARING TOGETHER

➤ Do you know what happens to leaves on trees in the fall? They turn colors and fall to the ground. Why do you think leaves fall from trees? Do you like the fall? What do you like about fall?

➤ Show the children several leaves. Let's look at these leaves together. Which leaf is your favorite? Why? How are these leaves different? How are these leaves alike?

WORKING TOGETHER

Invite the children to make several leaf rubbings. Place the leaves and paperless crayons on a work table within easy reach of the children. Give each child a sheet of white drawing paper and encourage him or her to choose a leaf for a rubbing. Then place the sheets of paper over the leaves. Show the children how to hold the papers firmly with one hand and then gently rub the sides of the paperless crayons over the papers to reveal the details of the leaves underneath. Display the children's leaf rubbings on a bulletin board labeled "Signs of Fall."

Fall Fruits and Vegetables

MATERIALS

- ➤ pictures of a variety of fruits and vegetables (or you may bring fresh fruits and vegetables from home)

- ➤ small paper plates

- ➤ glue

- ➤ small construction-paper squares, primarily red, orange, and yellow

- ➤ scissors

- ➤ marking pens or crayons

SHARING TOGETHER

➤ Show the children several pictures of a variety of fruits and vegetables. Or, you may want to show the children several fresh fruits and vegetables. Name some vegetables that grow in gardens. Does your family have a garden at home? What do you grow in your garden?

➤ What is your favorite fruit or vegetable? What color is your favorite fruit or vegetable?

WORKING TOGETHER

Talk about the fall harvest season with the children. Name some fruits and vegetables the children may not be familiar with, such as squash or peppers. If possible, bring a variety of fruits and vegetables to class to show the children. Then invite the children to make models of some fruits and vegetables. Give each child a paper plate. Place the other materials listed on page 10 on a work table within easy reach of the children. Encourage the children to choose the color of their favorite fruit or vegetable and glue construction-paper squares of that color all over both sides of their paper plates in an overlapping pattern—red squares for apples, orange squares for oranges or pumpkins, yellow squares for grapefruit, purple squares for eggplant, and so on. Invite the children to add special details using marking pens or crayons. Arrange the finished fruits and vegetables in a fall basket or on a tray and display them in the classroom.

Shopping Time

MATERIALS

➤ pictures of fruits and vegetables (glued onto index cards)

➤ grocery bag

SHARING TOGETHER

➤ Can you tell me the name of your favorite fruit? Can you tell me the name of your favorite vegetable? Do you know the season when most fruits and vegetables are picked?

➤ Do you ever go to the store with your parents to shop for food? How do you help your parents shop for food? Do you pick out your own fruits and vegetables? Which fruits do you pick? Which vegetables?

WORKING TOGETHER

Invite the children to sit together with you in a circle on the floor in a carpeted area. Have each child choose a picture of a fruit or vegetable, such as an apple, banana, carrot, turnip, and so on. Help the children identify each picture. Then select one child to role-play a "shopper." Invite the "shopper" to stand in the middle of the circle with a grocery bag and say, "I am looking for a juicy fruit and a fresh vegetable to take home to eat." Then have the "shopper" name one of the pictured fruits and one of the pictured vegetables. The children holding the pictures of these fruits and vegetables must quickly exchange places before the "shopper" can get to one of their seats. The child left without a place to sit becomes the next "shopper" and the game continues.

Printed Insects

MATERIALS

- ink pads
- white paper
- construction paper
- glue
- thin marking pens
- hand lenses
- warm, soapy water

SHARING TOGETHER

➤ Let's name some insects that we see in the fall. Do some of these insects fly? Which insects fly? Do some of these insects crawl? Which insects crawl? Which is your favorite insect?

➤ Look at the tips of your fingers. Can you see tiny lines on your fingertips? (Show the children the lines on their fingertips, if necessary.) Did you know that we all have special lines on our fingers? Everyone's lines are different. These lines are called *fingerprints*.

WORKING TOGETHER

Make prints of the children's fingertips by helping the children press their fingers on ink pads and then press their fingers on sheets of white paper. Be sure to let parents know about this activity in advance. Have warm, soapy water on hand to wash the children's hands thoroughly after they make their prints. Then encourage the children to use hand lenses to examine and then compare their own fingerprints with the fingerprints of others.

Invite the children to make insects from their fingerprints. Show the children how to use marking pens to draw details, such as circles for eyes, wavy lines for legs, and so on, to create fun fall insects. Frame the children's fingerprint insects by gluing the pictures on sheets of construction paper. Display the fingerprint insects on a bulletin board labeled "Signs of Fall."

LEARNING ABOUT MYSELF

FALL marks the beginning of a new school year filled with opportunities for social, emotional, physical, and intellectual growth. The young learner's awareness of self is an important basis for further learning. In these fall activities, the children learn to identify their own unique personal physical features, recognize and print their names, and handle important daily tasks, such as zipping and buttoning.

Self-Portraits

MATERIALS

- hand mirrors
- plastic lids
- felt circles in a variety of colors (cut to fit the plastic lids)
- glue
- yarn (yellow, black, brown, and red)
- felt scraps
- scissors
- pipe cleaners
- paper punch
- marking pens (optional)

SHARING TOGETHER

➤ Can you tell me what color your eyes are? What color is your hair? Raise your hand if you have freckles on your face. How many of you have curly black hair? How many of you have pretty black eyes? Do you have a tongue? Let's see all your tongues!

➤ When is the last time you made a new friend? Look at the child sitting next to you. Do you look the same? How? Do you look different? How?

WORKING TOGETHER

Invite the children to look at themselves in a hand mirror. Have the children touch and feel the shapes of their faces, noses, and mouths. Ask the children to note the colors of their eyes and hair as well. Ask the children to identify how they are like other children and how they are different, too. Discuss the similarities and differences. Explain to the children that although we are all alike in some ways, we are all different, too.

Invite the children to make self-portraits. Give each child a plastic lid and a felt circle. Place the other materials listed on page 16 on a work table within easy reach of the children. Encourage the children to glue the felt circles on the lids. Then help the children cut and glue felt pieces on the felt-covered lids to create facial features similar to the features of their own faces. Or, the children may draw facial features with marking pens, if desired. Help the children cut pieces of yarn that match the color of their own hair to glue on the lids as well. Punch a hole near the top of each plastic lid using a paper punch. Show the children how to insert pipe cleaners through the holes and then bend them to make hangers. Invite the children to take their self-portraits home to display in their bedrooms. Or, display the children's self-portraits on a bulletin board labeled "Me in the Fall!"

Traces of Me

MATERIALS

➤ large sheets of butcher paper (cut in child-size lengths)

➤ crayons

➤ marking pens

➤ scissors

➤ tape

SHARING TOGETHER

➤ Can you point to your arms? Legs? Hands? Feet? Elbows? How many toes (fingers, eyes, ears, knees, and so on) do you have? How do these body parts help you move? Let's move our bodies using our arms. Now let's move our bodies with our legs. We can move pretty far with our legs, can't we? How can we move with our knees (and so on)?

➤ School usually starts in the fall. Have you met some new friends this fall? Let's say hello to someone new. Can you say hello to the person next to you? Let's try it together.

WORKING TOGETHER

Invite the children to make models of themselves on paper. Have the children take turns lying very still on large sheets of butcher paper. Ask adult volunteers to trace around the children's body shapes with marking pens. Cut out each child's shape. Then encourage the children to use crayons to draw and color hair, facial features, and clothing on their body outlines to match their own physical features. Help the children write their names on their body shapes. Fold the body shapes into sitting positions and then tape them in each child's chair for a fall display at school.

My Silhouette

MATERIALS

➤ white, brown, and tan construction paper

➤ masking tape

➤ scissors

➤ overhead projector (or large flashlight or lamp)

➤ marking pens or crayons

➤ glue (optional)

➤ black construction paper (optional)

SHARING TOGETHER

➤ What is a shadow? Do you have a shadow? Let's see if we can
see our shadows. (Take the children outside, if possible.) Did
you know that the sun helps make your shadow? Does your
shadow look like you? Does your shadow move when you do?
Let's make our shadows move together.

WORKING TOGETHER

Invite the children to make silhouettes of themselves. Ask the
children to take turns sitting sideways in front of an overhead
projector light. Or, use a large flashlight or lamp if an overhead
projector is not available. Have adult volunteers trace around the
children's silhouettes that are cast onto white, brown, or tan sheets
of construction paper taped to the wall. Then ask the volunteers to
help the children cut their silhouettes from the white, brown, or tan
paper. Encourage the children to use marking pens or crayons to
draw facial features and fall clothing details on the silhouettes that
are similar to their own physical features. Then, if desired, show
the children how to glue their finished silhouettes on black
construction paper to make a frame. Display the silhouettes on a
bulletin board labeled "Me in the Fall!"

Printing Practice

MATERIALS

➤ large, flat trays

➤ sand, salt, or sugar

➤ glue

➤ pumpkins cut from orange construction paper

SHARING TOGETHER

➤ Can you trace your name on the floor? Let's try it together. Can you trace your name on the wall? Let's pretend to trace our names on the wall.

➤ What letter of the alphabet do you like best? Why is this letter your favorite? Let's practice writing your favorite letters together.

WORKING TOGETHER

Invite the children to practice printing their names or a favorite letter. Ask the children to help you cover the bottoms of several flat trays with sand, salt, or sugar. Encourage the children to trace their names or letters in the sand, salt, or sugar using their index fingers. Suggest to the children that they practice tracing their names or letters at different times throughout the day.

As an extension to this activity, help the children trace their names or letters with glue on orange paper pumpkins. Then sprinkle sand, salt, or sugar over the glue. After the glue is dry, shake off the excess sand, salt, or sugar to reveal the children's names or letters. Display the fall pumpkin prints on a Sharing Wall in the classroom.

Nametags

MATERIALS

➤ fall leaves cut from tagboard or stiff paper

➤ glue

➤ glitter

➤ newspaper

➤ tape

SHARING TOGETHER

➤ Let's all stand together in a circle. Do you know everybody's name in the circle? Let's go around the circle and say our names. (Start with yourself, then ask each child to say his or her name as you go around the circle.)

➤ Do you know what a nametag is? Why do you think people wear nametags? What things at home have your name on them? What things at school have your name on them?

WORKING TOGETHER

Invite the children to make their own special fall nametags. Help the children print their names with glue on one or more tagboard fall leaves, spacing the letters on each nametag so the glue does not touch. Then place the nametags on newspaper and sprinkle glitter over the glue (excess glitter may be reused). Encourage the children to tape their fall nametags on school boxes, chairs, or lockers, or on their beds, bedroom doors, or other personal items at home. Or, pin the children's fall nametags on a "Me in the Fall!" bulletin board.

Shining Shoes

MATERIALS

➤ several pairs of shoes (ask children to bring a pair of dress shoes from home)

➤ polishing cloth

➤ non-toxic, mild shoe polish (optional)

SHARING TOGETHER

➤ What kinds of shoes do you wear in the fall? Do you wear
sandals in the fall? Do you wear slippers in the fall? Do you
wear snow boots in the fall? What kind of shoes are you
wearing today? How do you take care of your shoes? Have you
ever polished a pair of shoes? Whose shoes did you polish?

WORKING TOGETHER

Invite the children to polish a pair of shoes. Ask the children to
gather around a low table. Have each child tuck any shoelaces
inside each of their shoes and then take turns polishing the shoes
with a polishing cloth. You may want to purchase a non-toxic, mild
polish for the children to use as well. Ask the children to see how
clean and shiny they can get their shoes. Talk about other ways
children can take care of their belongings, such as hanging up
their clothes, putting toys away, and so on.

As an alternative activity, sponsor a shoe polishing fund-raiser.
Invite parents and other classes to bring their shoes to school for
polishing. Charge a nickel or dime for each pair of shoes polished
and use the money to buy something special for the classroom. Or,
donate the money to a charity.

Folding Clothes

MATERIALS

➤ an assortment of
clothes—socks,
pajamas, T-shirts,
shorts or long
pants, towels,
sheets, and
washcloths

➤ laundry basket

SHARING TOGETHER

➤ What kinds of clothes do you wear in the fall? Is it cooler in the fall than in the summer? Do you wear T-shirts in the fall? Do you wear a jacket in the fall? Do you wear long pants in the fall?

➤ What jobs do you do at home to help your family? Do you help your parents do the laundry? Do you do the dishes? What else do you do to help your mom or dad?

WORKING TOGETHER

Ask the children if they ever help their parents fold the laundry at home. Invite the children to watch carefully as you fold several different clothing items from a laundry basket. Then encourage the children to practice folding the different laundry items, matching the socks before folding them together. Encourage the children to stack the folded clothes neatly back in the laundry basket. Add larger items for the children to fold, too, such as beach towels, table cloths, or sheets, that encourage children to work together.

Button, Snap, and Zip

MATERIALS

➤ lace shoes

➤ snow boots with buckles

➤ dress shirts

➤ jackets with zippers

➤ jeans or coats with snaps

➤ large box

➤ posterboard

➤ tacks

SHARING TOGETHER

➤ Do you sometimes wear a coat or jacket in the fall? Can you pretend to zip up your coat? Let's try it together. Can you pretend to button up your jacket? Now let's pretend to lace our shoes.

WORKING TOGETHER

Before beginning this activity, place the materials listed in a large box or tack to posterboard. Invite the children to practice the skills for dressing by lacing, buckling, buttoning, zipping, or snapping the items in the box or on the board. Have the children help one another as needed, or ask an adult volunteer to help. Store the items in a learning center for the children to work with during independent time.

MAKING NEW FRIENDS

FALL is a time when children begin to feel more comfortable with one another as they learn to work together in groups. Through fall friendship activities, the children learn the names of their classmates, recognize and read their own names in print, become aware of the unique physical characteristics of others, and discover the importance of listening carefully to one another.

A Friendship Game

MATERIALS

➤ a bell
➤ crayons
➤ white paper
➤ name cards

Make New Fall Friends

Shelby

William

Vicky

Danielle

SHARING TOGETHER

➤ Do you know how to make friends? What do you say to someone when you want to be friends? Do you tell your new friend your name? Can you tell me the name of one of your friends?

➤ Would you please stand up if your name is (Joe)? Would you please stand up if your hair is (brown)? Stand up if your eyes are (blue). (Continue the game until all children have been included.)

WORKING TOGETHER

Divide the class into pairs. Invite the children to introduce themselves to each other by saying "Hello, my name is (Susan) and I am happy to be your friend." Explain to the children that when you ring a bell, they should switch partners and meet someone new. Then encourage the children to draw pictures of their new friends on sheets of white paper. Print the children's names on name cards to place beside the drawings. Display the drawings on a bulletin board labeled "Make New Fall Friends." Then invite the children to take their drawings home to share with family members.

A Friendship Chain

MATERIALS

➤ 2" x 6" strips of construction paper

➤ marking pens or crayons

➤ stapler or tape

➤ name cards (print each child's name on a card)

SHARING TOGETHER

➤ How do you show someone that you want them to be your friend? What nice things do you do for your friends? How do you like to be treated by your friends?

➤ Do you like to play with your friends? Do you like to help your friends? How? Do you know how to make friends? How are you different than your friends? Stand up if you have black hair. Stand up if you have dark eyes. Raise your hand if you have red hair. How are we the same as our friends?

WORKING TOGETHER

Before starting this activity, print each child's name on a card. Then invite the children to copy their names on strips of construction paper, using the name cards as models. Help the children tape or staple their name strips together to form a long friendship chain. Encourage the children to work together. Ask each child to hold a section of the chain and help you drape the chain in the classroom. Or, display the chain on a friendship bulletin board to remind everyone of the importance of fall friendships.

Let's Make New Friends

MATERIALS

➤ construction-
   paper patterns of
   children

➤ white paper

➤ scissors

➤ crayons or
   marking pens

➤ tape

SHARING TOGETHER

➤ Do you like to make new friends? Why? What special things do you do with your friends?

➤ Can you tell me the name of a friend who is wearing (blue) today? What color are the eyes of the friend sitting next to you? Ask the friend sitting next to you what his or her favorite food is.

WORKING TOGETHER

Before beginning this activity, cut several children shapes from construction paper. Then invite the children to trace around the construction-paper patterns on sheets of white paper. The children may then cut out the patterns they trace, asking for help as needed. Divide the class into pairs. Encourage children to draw the features and details of their partners on the patterns. Tape the patterns together at the hands to make a friendship chain to display in the classroom or on a fall friendship bulletin board.

Do As I Say

MATERIALS

➤ none

SHARING TOGETHER

➤ Can you stand on your tiptoes? Let's try it together. Can you clap your hands? Let's clap our hands three times. Can you twirl around? Let's see you twirl around.

➤ What games do you like to play in the fall? Have you ever played "Simon Says"? Who knows how to play? Who would like to play "Simon Says"?

WORKING TOGETHER

Ask the children to follow several directions, such as "Touch your nose," "Touch your toes," and "Touch your mouth." Challenge the children to follow more complex directions, such as "Touch your knees twice and then touch your head." When children are ready, invite one child to be the leader and give the other children directions. Encourage the children to take turns being the leader and giving directions for their friends to follow. Make sure each child gets a chance to be the leader.

EXPLORING FALL THROUGH MY SENSES

ENCOURAGING children to use their senses helps them uncover rich information about the fall season. The following activities invite the children to discover their special sense organs, smells of different substances, flavors of various foods, different textures, similar sounds, and visual changes in their world.

A Sensible Game

MATERIALS

➤ pictures of eyes, nose, mouth, ears, and hands

➤ pictures of fall-related items that may be seen, smelled, tasted, heard, and touched

➤ large index cards

➤ glue

➤ drawing paper

➤ crayons

SHARING TOGETHER

➤ Did you know that you have five senses? They are hearing, tasting, feeling, seeing, and smelling. What part of your body do you use to smell a rose? To taste ice cream? To see a rainbow? To feel a soft blanket? To hear the rain?

➤ What is your favorite taste? What is your favorite smell? What things do you like to touch? What sounds do you like to hear? What do you like to see in the fall?

WORKING TOGETHER

Before beginning this activity, mount each of the pictures of the eyes, nose, mouth, ears, and hands, as well as the fall-related items, on large index cards. Invite the children to match the pictures of the eyes, nose, mouth, ears, and hands with the fall-related pictures showing when the appropriate senses are used. Then take the children on a fall walk. Ask the children to notice the fall things around them with all of their senses (except taste). Be sure to obtain signed field-trip permission slips from the children's parents if you plan on leaving the school grounds. When you return to the classroom, discuss all of the things the children touched, smelled, heard, and saw on their walk. Then encourage the children to draw pictures of their favorite fall sights, smells, sounds, tastes, and textures. Store the cards in a learning center for the children to use during independent time.

Tasting and Smelling

MATERIALS

➤ apples, oranges, lemons, grapes, and other fruits

➤ 2 trays

➤ blindfold

➤ napkins

➤ knife (for adult use only)

SHARING TOGETHER

➤ What are some of your favorite smells? Do you like the smell of fruits in the fall? What does your nose smell at a bakery? What other smells do you like?

➤ What are some of your favorite foods to taste? What is your favorite flavor of icing on a cake? How might you guess what you are having for dinner without even opening your eyes?

WORKING TOGETHER

Before beginning this activity, cut several fruits into small pieces. Divide the pieces in half and put half of the fruit pieces aside on a tray. Place the other half of the fruit pieces on another tray on a work table. Invite the children to identify fruits with their sense of smell. Loosely blindfold one child at a time and help him or her smell a small piece of one of the fruits. Then challenge the child, still blindfolded, to lean over the tray containing an assortment of different fruits and sniff to find a matching piece. When the child has identified the matching fruit, remove the matching pieces from the tray and place them on napkins. Continue the activity until all of the children have had a chance to match the fruits using their sense of smell. Then, invite the children to sample the fruit pieces on the tray set aside earlier.

The Smelling Game

MATERIALS

➤ 8 baby food jars

➤ contact paper

➤ coffee

➤ tea

➤ cinnamon

➤ cloves

➤ blindfold (optional)

SHARING TOGETHER

➤ How do the leaves smell in the fall? How does the air smell? Have you ever smelled wood or leaves burning in the fall? What other smells do you notice in the fall?

➤ What is your favorite kitchen smell? Do you like to bake things? Do you like the smell of cookies baking? What other cooking smells do you like?

WORKING TOGETHER

Before beginning this activity, cover the sides of the baby food jars with contact paper so the children cannot see the contents. Fill the jars with small amounts of coffee, tea, cinnamon, and cloves, using two jars for each substance. Then invite the children, one at a time, to remove the lids from one set of the baby food jars filled with spices and smell each of the substances inside. Encourage the children to close their eyes (or loosely blindfold each child) and use their sense of smell to match the spices with the other set of bottles that contain the same spices. Help the children replace the proper lids on each bottle. Be sure to rearrange the spice bottles every time after each child has had a turn.

Fabric Sort

MATERIALS

➤ samples of different textured fabrics (silk, corduroy, linen, terry cloth, burlap, velvet, cotton, and so on)

➤ index cards

➤ glue

➤ blindfold

SHARING TOGETHER

➤ What parts of your body do you use to tell you how things feel (fingers, skin)? Have you ever touched a kitten? How does a kitten's fur feel? Have you ever felt a tree trunk? How does a tree feel?

➤ Can you name something that feels fuzzy? How about something that feels rough? Name something that feels smooth. What feels bumpy?

WORKING TOGETHER

Before beginning this activity, glue fabric pieces of the same size on index cards—two cards for each texture. Then invite the children to spread out all of the fabric sample cards and match the fabrics that feel the same—bumpy, smooth, rough, and so on. Discuss the texture of each type of material with the children after all of the matches have been made. Encourage the children to try the activity again wearing a blindfold and using only their sense of touch.

As an extension to this activity, encourage the children to collect fall nature items to sort according to textures. Store the items in a learning center for the children to sort during independent time.

Touch and Tell

MATERIALS

➤ small pictures of something hard and something soft

➤ two paper plates

➤ fall objects that are hard and soft, such as bark, feathers, nuts, rocks, leaves, moss, and so on

➤ glue

SHARING TOGETHER

➤ What feels soft? Do you know what moss is? Moss is a plant that grows on trees and rocks. (Show the children some moss.) Do you think moss feels soft or hard? Let's feel it together. Did you guess correctly?

➤ What feels hard? Can you name something that is hard? Can you name something that is soft?

WORKING TOGETHER

Before beginning this activity, print "Hard" on one paper plate and "Soft" on the other. Draw or glue a picture on each plate of a sample of each word as well. Place the hard and soft fall objects on a work table. Then invite the children to look at the plates and identify the words and their meanings. Encourage the children to feel the different items on the table carefully and then place the items on the appropriate plates. Be sure each child gets a chance to sort the items. Store the materials in a learning center for the children to work with during independent time.

Match a Sound

MATERIALS

➤ jars of the same size and shape

➤ materials to put into the jars, such as rice, small beans, dirt, marbles, pennies, flour, popcorn, and so on

➤ contact paper

SHARING TOGETHER

➤ What makes a loud sound? Is a whisper a loud sound? How about an airplane flying overhead? What makes a soft sound? How about a high sound? What makes a low sound?

➤ What part of your body helps you hear sounds? What special sounds do you hear in the fall (raking leaves, wind, leaves blowing on the ground)?

WORKING TOGETHER

Before beginning this activity, cover the sides of the jars with contact paper so the children cannot see the contents. Fill the containers half full with the materials (you will need two jars for each substance) and then place the lids on tightly. Invite the children to shake the jars containing the various materials and guess what is inside. Then challenge the children to match the containers by the sounds they make. Help the children remove the lids to check their predictions after all matches have been made. Store the jars in a learning center for the children to work with during independent time.

Take a Good Look

MATERIALS

➤ at least 10 familiar objects, such as a leaf, spoon, scissors, pen, clothespin, toothpick, and so on

➤ towel

➤ tray

SHARING TOGETHER

➤ What do you see outside in the fall? Do you see snow? Do you see leaves? What is different about the leaves in the fall compared to the leaves in the spring or summer?

➤ What part of your body helps you see? What is (red and round) in the classroom? Point out something that is (blue and square) in the classroom. (Continue to describe things in the classroom by size and color.)

WORKING TOGETHER

Arrange a few of the objects listed on a tray. Invite the children to study and identify each item. Remind the children to look carefully at each item in order to remember as many items on the tray as they can. Then cover the tray of items with a towel and ask the children to recall as many items on the tray as possible. Remove the towel and discuss which items, if any, were forgotten. Add more items to the tray for a greater challenge.

As an extension of this activity, cover the tray and remove one object. Encourage the children to identify which item was removed.

ENJOYING SPECIAL FALL DAYS

CHILDREN learn about their heritage and the heritage of others by celebrating holidays with family and friends. During the special fall activities in this section, children explore customs associated with Halloween and Thanksgiving, prepare and eat holiday foods, and make holiday decorations.

Halloween Treat Bag

MATERIALS

➤ medium-size brown paper bags

➤ 2" wide strips of orange or black construction paper

➤ marking pens or crayons

➤ stapler

SHARING TOGETHER

➤ Do you like to get treats from your neighbors on Halloween? What do you do when you visit your neighbors on Halloween? Do you wear a costume? What costume do you wear?

➤ What things remind you of Halloween (bats, witches, pumpkins, ghosts)? How do you carry your treats from door-to-door when you visit your neighbors on Halloween?

WORKING TOGETHER

Invite the children to make special Halloween treat bags. Give each child a brown paper bag. Then invite the children to use marking pens or crayons to decorate the paper bags. Help the children draw Halloween symbols, such as cats, pumpkins, moons, stars, candles, bats, ghosts, and so on. Staple 2″ wide strips of orange or black construction paper to the tops of the bags for handles. Encourage the children to use their decorated Halloween bags to collect treats at the classroom door. Give the children a healthy treat! Or, arrange with other classrooms to exchange treats on Halloween.

Halloween Make-Believe

MATERIALS

➤ a large box containing clothes, shoes, costume jewelry, wigs, hats, sunglasses, false beards, and other dress-up items

SHARING TOGETHER

➤ Do you like to play in the dress-up center? Who or what do you like to be when you dress up? Do you play dress-up at home?

➤ What are some Halloween costumes you like to wear? Who or what do you want to be on Halloween? Do you have a favorite TV star you would like to dress up as on Halloween? Who?

WORKING TOGETHER

Before beginning this activity, send a note home asking parents to contribute items to the class for a dress-up center—old shoes, clothing, costume jewelry, and so on. Make sure there is enough clothing and props for each child to use. Then invite the children to create their own costumes using dress-up clothing and accessories. Encourage the children to act out pretend people for the class to guess. Have a costume parade throughout the school, if possible.

A Ghostly Treat

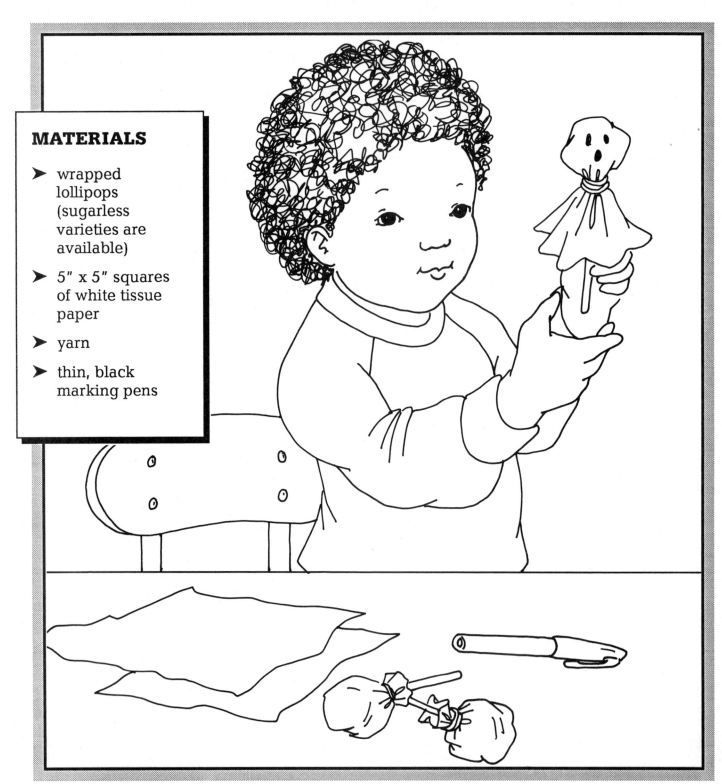

MATERIALS

➤ wrapped lollipops (sugarless varieties are available)

➤ 5" x 5" squares of white tissue paper

➤ yarn

➤ thin, black marking pens

SHARING TOGETHER

➤ What are your favorite Halloween costumes? Have you ever seen anyone dressed as a ghost on Halloween? What other costumes do you see on Halloween? Do you like to get treats on Halloween? What are some of your favorite Halloween treats?

WORKING TOGETHER

Give each child a wrapped lollipop and a tissue-paper square. Invite the children to make a lollipop ghost! Show the children how to cover the lollipop with the tissue square and then secure the tissue square in place by tying yarn around the lollipop base. Encourage the children to use marking pens to draw facial features on the lollipop's head. Join the children in enjoying the ghostly treats for a snack!

Jack-o'-Lantern Puzzles

MATERIALS

➤ paper plates

➤ orange construction paper or tissue paper (cut into tiny pieces)

➤ black marking pens or crayons

➤ scissors

➤ envelopes

SHARING TOGETHER

➤ What shape is a pumpkin? Is a pumpkin square? Is a pumpkin shaped like a circle? What can you do with a pumpkin? How do you make a jack-o'-lantern from a pumpkin?

➤ Have you ever made a jack-o'-lantern from a pumpkin? What did your jack-o'-lantern look like? Did it have a scary face? A happy face? A sad face? Let's try to make jack-o'-lantern faces with our own faces!

WORKING TOGETHER

Invite the children to make jack-o'-lantern puzzles. Give each child a paper plate. Ask the children to paste pieces of orange construction paper or tissue paper all over the fronts of their paper plates. Suggest to the children that they use black marking pens or crayons to draw jack-o'-lantern faces on the plates. Then help the children section off the plates on the back sides and cut the plates into puzzle pieces. Encourage the children to enjoy putting their jack-o'-lantern puzzles together. Place each child's puzzle pieces in an envelope. Invite the children to take their jack-o'-lantern puzzles home to share with their families.

Pumpkin Treats

MATERIALS

➤ oranges
➤ raisins
➤ black gumdrops
➤ butter knives

SHARING TOGETHER

➤ What colors remind you of Halloween? Does orange remind you of Halloween? What about black? Name some things that are orange. Name some things that are black.

➤ Name some healthy Halloween treats. What are your favorite treats? Would an orange make a good Halloween treat?

WORKING TOGETHER

Invite the children to make special Halloween treats using oranges. Ask the children to wash their hands and the oranges thoroughly. Place the other materials listed on page 62 on a work table within easy reach of the children. Help the children cut the raisins in half and then show the children how to use them to create jack-o'-lantern faces (the cut sides stick to the oranges). Then encourage the children to cut the tops off black gumdrops and stick them on the tops of the oranges for stems. Use the "jack-o'-lanterns" as centerpieces that may then be eaten for healthy Halloween snacks.

Turkey Decorations

MATERIALS

➤ picture of a turkey

➤ large, round pinecones

➤ turkey head patterns cut from red construction paper

➤ turkey feathers cut from various colors of construction paper

➤ thin marking pens

➤ glue

SHARING TOGETHER

➤ What bird has a large body, says "Gobble, Gobble," and is often part of a Thanksgiving meal? Have you ever seen a turkey? Where? Does a turkey have fur or feathers? Let's look at a picture of a turkey. What colors do you see on a turkey? Let's pretend we are turkeys. Don't forget to "Gobble"!

➤ What else do you eat at your house on Thanksgiving? Do you eat corn on Thanksgiving? How about potatoes? Discuss briefly the first Thanksgiving.

WORKING TOGETHER

Invite the children to make pinecone turkey decorations. Place the materials listed on page 64 on a work table within easy reach of the children. Encourage the children to use marking pens to draw facial features on the red construction-paper turkey-head patterns, as well as details on the construction-paper feathers. Help the children put glue on the bases of the turkey necks and stick them into one end of each pinecone. Show the children how to put glue on the ends of the feathers and then stick several feathers into the opposite ends of the pinecones for tails. Invite the children to take their pinecone turkeys home to use as Thanksgiving table decorations.

Thanksgiving Plaques

MATERIALS

➤ paper plates

➤ marking pens or crayons

SHARING TOGETHER

➤ What is special about Thanksgiving? What things are you thankful for on Thanksgiving? What people are you thankful for?

➤ How can you show your family that you love them? Do you help your parents around the house? Are you helpful to your brothers and sisters? Are there other ways you show your family that you love them? How?

WORKING TOGETHER

Invite the children to make Thanksgiving plaques. Use a marking pen to divide paper plates into four equal sections. Give each child a sectioned plate. Invite the children to draw pictures on the plates of things and people they are thankful for—one picture for each section. Encourage the children to decorate the rippled edges of the plates with bright colors to make frames. Then invite the children to share information about their Thanksgiving plaque drawings with the rest of the class. Display the children's finished plaques in the classroom or on a "We Are Thankful for..." bulletin-board display.

Thanksgiving Centerpieces

MATERIALS

➤ fruit patterns cut from tagboard

➤ 2" wide strips of cardboard

➤ shoeboxes (children bring from home)

➤ brown wrapping paper

➤ different colors of construction paper

➤ scissors

➤ glue

➤ marking pens or crayons

➤ stapler

SHARING TOGETHER

➤ What foods do you eat at Thanksgiving? Do you eat a lot of fruits and vegetables? What kinds? What is your favorite Thanksgiving food? What is your favorite fruit?

➤ Who eats your Thanksgiving meal with you? Do you have Thanksgiving with your parents? Who else do you share Thanksgiving dinner with?

WORKING TOGETHER

Before beginning this activity, cut fruit patterns from tagboard for the children to trace around. Then invite the children to make special Thanksgiving centerpieces. Help the children cover shoeboxes with brown wrapping paper. Be sure to cover the insides of the shoeboxes with paper as well. Staple cardboard strips to the shoeboxes for handles. Show the children how to draw lines on the brown wrapping paper to resemble strips on a basket. Invite the children to trace around the tagboard fruit patterns on construction paper. Then help the children cut out the shapes of the different fruits and place the paper fruits inside the baskets. Encourage the children to take the baskets home and then fill their fruit baskets with real fruits for Thanksgiving dinner.

Turkey Table Favors

MATERIALS

➤ individual egg carton sections

➤ brown tempera paint

➤ paintbrushes

➤ turkey head patterns cut from red construction paper

➤ turkey tail-feather patterns cut from various colors of construction paper

➤ stapler

➤ marking pens

➤ candy corn

➤ small paper bags

➤ knife (for adult use only)

SHARING TOGETHER

➤ Do you help your family set the table at mealtimes? How do you help? What do you set on the table (plates, forks, spoons, glasses, and so on)?

WORKING TOGETHER

Invite the children to make special Thanksgiving table favors. Give the children an egg carton section for each member of his or her family. Then have the children paint the sides and bottoms of the egg carton sections with brown tempera paint. Remind the children to wear paint shirts or smocks. Encourage the children to use marking pens to draw details on red construction-paper turkey heads and different colors of construction-paper feathers. Help the children staple several tail feathers to one side of each egg cup. Make slits in the opposite sides of each egg cup to insert the turkey head patterns. Then fill the egg cups with candy corn. Carefully pack each child's favors in a small brown paper bag. Invite the children to take the turkey table favors home to place on the table beside each family member's place on Thanksgiving Day.

EXPLORING FALL THROUGH ART

ART is a fun, productive way of learning about the fall season. Using different materials, the children can fingerpaint, make fall flowers, and learn to lace.

Fingerpainting

MATERIALS

➤ packages of powdered drink mixes (orange, cherry, and grape)

➤ egg cartons

➤ white paper

➤ water

SHARING TOGETHER

➤ What do you see outside in the fall? Do you see snow? What happens to the leaves in the fall? What colors do you see outside in the fall? Can you name some things outside that are red in the fall (leaves, apples)? How about some things that are orange (leaves, pumpkins)?

➤ Have you ever painted with your fingers? What did you paint? How does it feel to paint with your fingers? Let's paint fall pictures together with our fingers.

WORKING TOGETHER

Place each kind of powdered drink mix into a separate egg carton section. Invite the children to help you mix the "fingerpaint" using their fingers. Blend a few drops of water into the mixes in each section until the mixtures are the consistency of fingerpaints. Give each child a sheet of white paper. Then drop large dabs of the mixtures on the sheets of paper. Encourage the children to fingerpaint fall objects. Discuss the different smells created by the various flavors of the powdered mixes. Display the children's fingerpaintings on a Sharing Wall in the classroom.

As an alternative activity, invite the children to "draw" with glue on sheets of paper and then sprinkle powdered mixes over the drawings. Have the children shake off the excess powder.

Fall Flowers

MATERIALS

➤ 9" x 12" brown or orange construction paper

➤ sheets of posterboard

➤ glue

➤ an assortment of dried fall flowers

➤ yarn or pipe cleaners

➤ stapler

➤ scissors

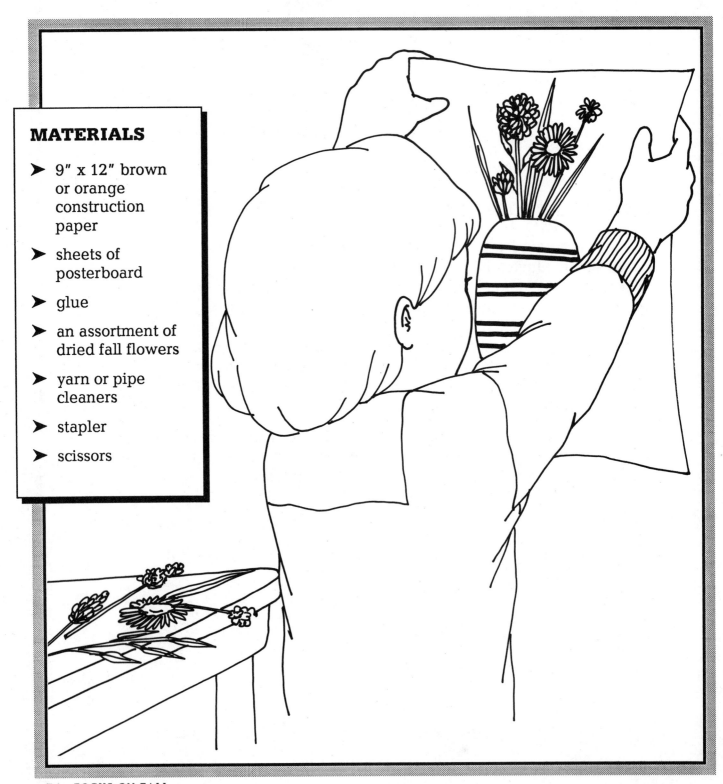